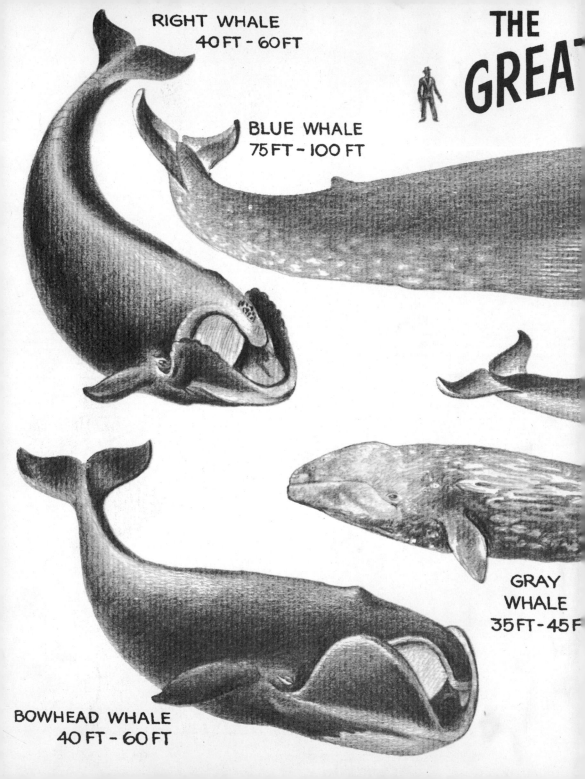

RIGHT WHALE
40 FT - 60 FT

BLUE WHALE
75 FT - 100 FT

THE
GREAT

BOWHEAD WHALE
40 FT - 60 FT

GRAY
WHALE
35 FT - 45 FT

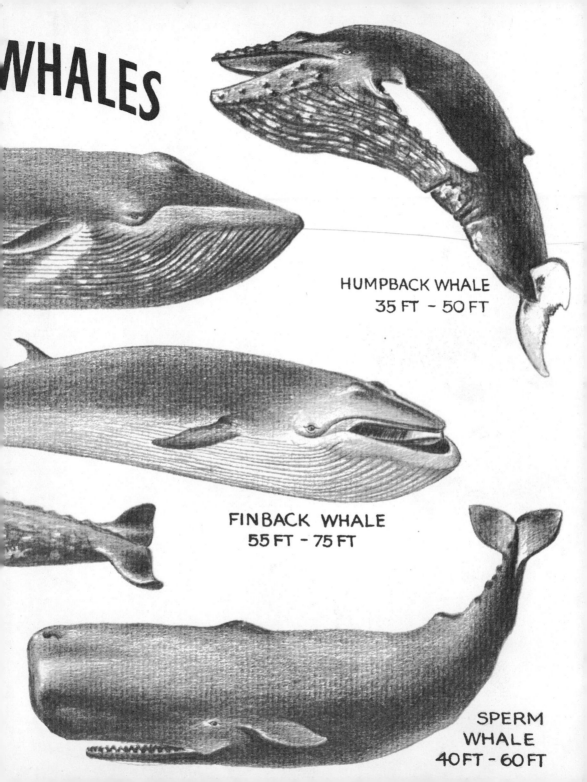

WHALES

HUMPBACK WHALE
35 FT - 50 FT

FINBACK WHALE
55 FT - 75 FT

SPERM
WHALE
40 FT - 60 FT

THE
GREAT WHALES

by HERBERT S. ZIM

illustrated by *James Gordon Irving*

WILLIAM MORROW & COMPANY, NEW YORK, 1951
Copyright 1951 by Herbert S. Zim. Printed in the U.S.A.

18 19 20

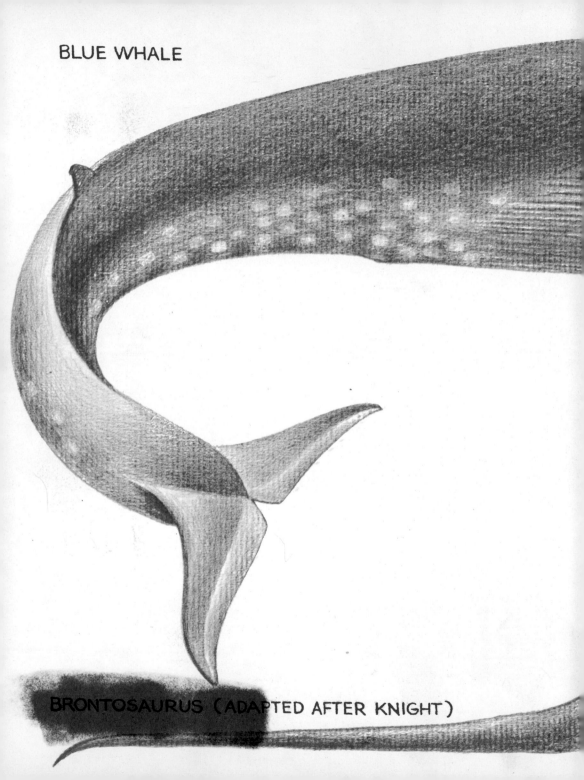

BLUE WHALE

BRONTOSAURUS (ADAPTED AFTER KNIGHT)

The great whales are the largest animals that have ever lived. No dinosaur, not even the giant brontosaurus, was as big.

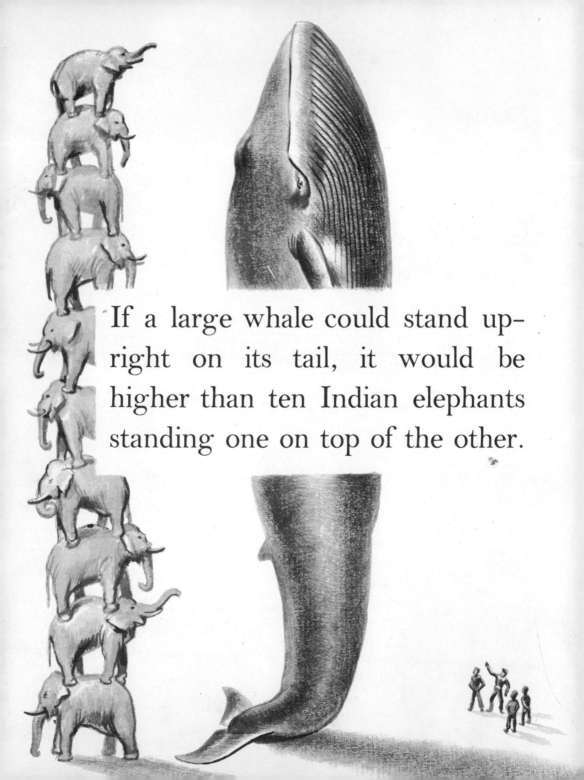

If a large whale could stand upright on its tail, it would be higher than ten Indian elephants standing one on top of the other.

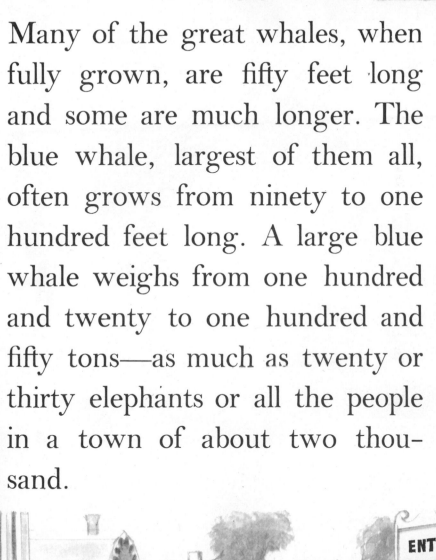

Many of the great whales, when fully grown, are fifty feet long and some are much longer. The blue whale, largest of them all, often grows from ninety to one hundred feet long. A large blue whale weighs from one hundred and twenty to one hundred and fifty tons—as much as twenty or thirty elephants or all the people in a town of about two thousand.

ENTERING
OCEAN ARBOR
MAINE
POPULATION 2051

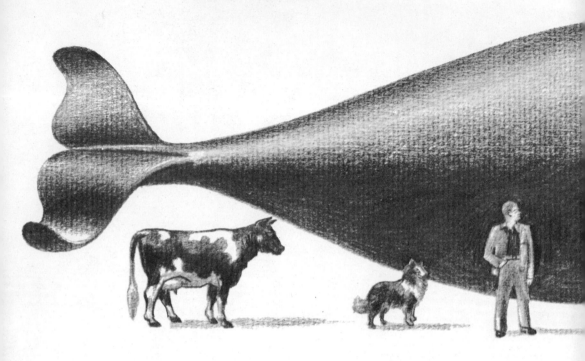

Whales are not fish. They belong to the same group of animals as cows, lions, dogs, and men. Whales are mammals and, like all mammals, they breathe air. They are warm-blooded, bear

their young alive, and nurse
them with milk. All mammals
are hairy, but the dark gray or
blackish skins of whales have no
hair. Only a few whiskers remain
to show that the ancestors of

whales were once hairy animals. These distant ancestors of whales were land animals. Of all the mammals which have returned from the land to live in the sea, like seals, sea lions, walruses, and manatees, none is as fit as the whale for life in the water.

Scientists do not know when, how, or why the remote ances-

MANATEE

PACIFIC WALRUS

NORTHERN
SEA LION

ALASKA FUR SEAL

tors of whales began their return to the sea. It must have been at least sixty million years ago. Millions of years ago the ocean covered much of what is now Alabama. In the rocks formed

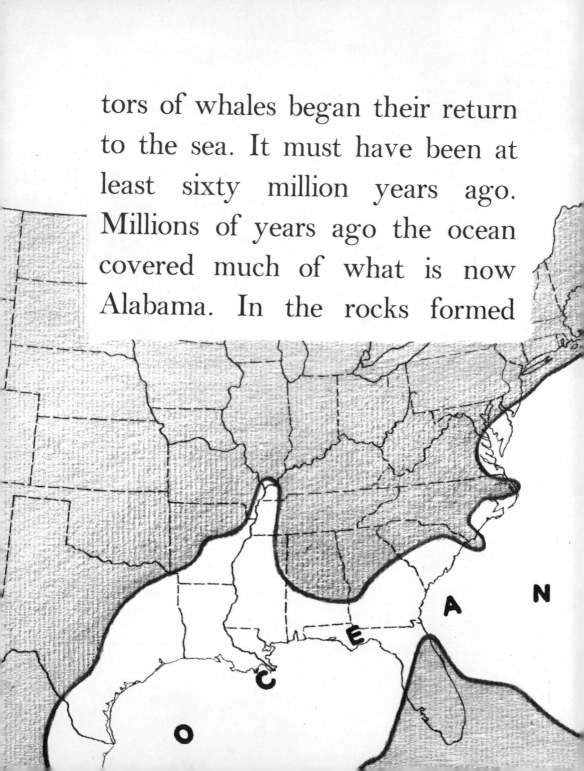

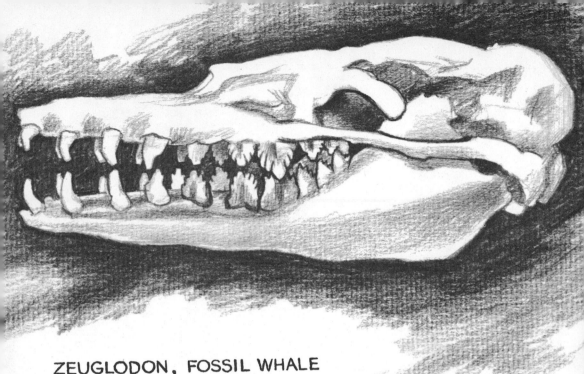

ZEUGLODON, FOSSIL WHALE

under that ocean scientists have found bones that came from a whalelike, slender, toothed mammal, some seventy feet long.

This animal looked like a sea serpent, but its bones show it

was a close relative of modern whales. All living whales are the descendants of this creature and others like it. Whales once lived

ZEUGLODON, FOSSIL WHALE
(ADAPTED AFTER KNIGHT)

and were common in all the oceans. Now they are not common except in the Pacific and in the waters around the poles.

SHAPES OF WHALES

SEI WHALE

HUMPBACK WHALE

The great whales are completely streamlined and well suited to water life. Their tapering shape and smooth hairless skin help them move through water with ease. Their bones are soft and spongy, making them light in weight and not very strong for their size. But since the whale's heavy body is supported by water, a strong skeleton is not as important as it is for a land mammal.

The bones of the whale's short neck are fused together. This gives more support to the huge head, which may be a quarter the size of the entire whale. But it also means that the whale cannot turn its head. This may not be much of a loss, since the whale's eyes are small and are set far back. Whales cannot see straight ahead and they cannot see as well in the air as they can under

GRAY WHALE

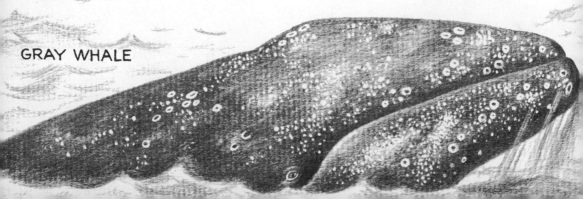

water. When they dive below five hundred feet, there is practically no light anyway. Whales shed greasy tears, which bathe their eyes and help protect them from the salt in the sea. Whales hear well in the water, but they have no ears outside their bodies, as we have, with which to hear

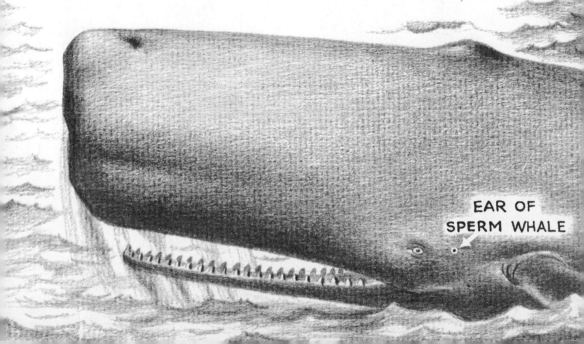

EAR OF SPERM WHALE

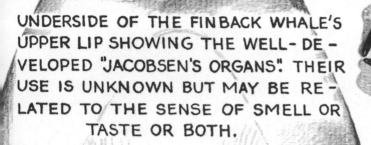

UNDERSIDE OF THE FINBACK WHALE'S UPPER LIP SHOWING THE WELL-DE- VELOPED "JACOBSEN'S ORGANS". THEIR USE IS UNKNOWN BUT MAY BE RE- LATED TO THE SENSE OF SMELL OR TASTE OR BOTH.

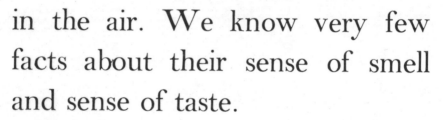

in the air. We know very few facts about their sense of smell and sense of taste.

Whales have lost the hind limbs their ancestors once had. Only a few small bones remain inside their bodies near the back- bone. The front legs or arms

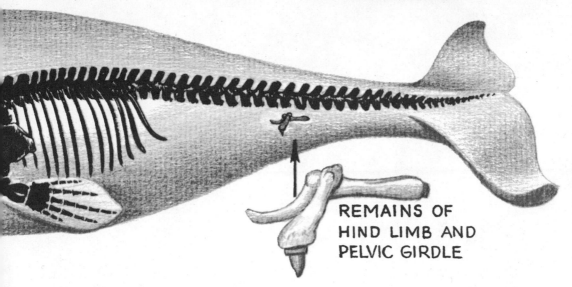

REMAINS OF
HIND LIMB AND
PELVIC GIRDLE

have changed to become the flippers which the whale uses in
balancing and steering. Inside
each flipper are the bones of the
whale's arm, hand, and five fin-
gers. Instead of a tail, a whale
has a pair of huge, thin, flat-
tened flukes. They are *horizontal*

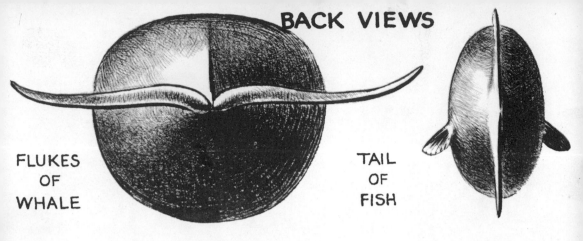

FLUKES
OF
WHALE

TAIL
OF
FISH

and move up and down. The tails of fishes are *vertical* and move from side to side.

The whale's flukes are its propeller. The up-and-down wiggle of the flukes gives the great whale speeds of five to ten miles an hour, though a frightened whale can go much faster. So can all

FLIPPER OF
RIGHT WHALE
SHOWING
INTERNAL
FIVE - FINGER
CONSTRUCTION

SIDE VIEWS

FLUKES OF WHALE

TAIL OF FISH

the smaller whales and dolphins, which have no trouble keeping up with most passenger ships.

COMMON DOLPHINS

Like other mammals, the whale has a four-chambered heart, a huge one that pumps the warm red blood around its body. The thick layer of fat or blubber beneath the skin protects the whale from the icy waters and preserves its body heat. This blubber, which is sometimes a foot or more thick, also serves to keep the whale alive when food is scarce. Walruses, seals, and other ocean mammals have blubber too, but not as much of it.

Whales must have air to breathe. Sooner or later they must come to the surface after they dive or sound. Whales often stay under ten or fifteen minutes. But a frightened or wounded whale may submerge for an hour or more before coming up to

breathe or blow. As soon as a whale reaches the surface, it exhales the carbon-dioxide-laden air in its lungs through its nostrils, which are on the top of its head. Then it breathes in fresh air, richer in oxygen.

HUMPBACK WHALE
SURFACING

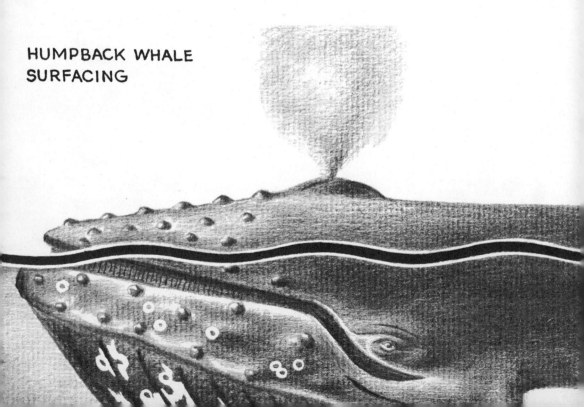

The warm air in the whale's lungs has become filled with water vapor. When the whale exhales, the warm water vapor forms a cloud in the cold air, just as your breath does on a winter's day. The whale's breath, blowing

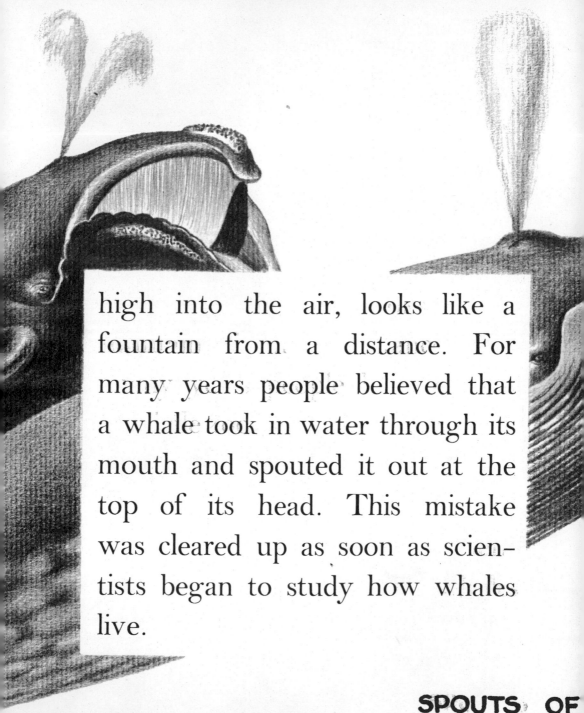

high into the air, looks like a fountain from a distance. For many years people believed that a whale took in water through its mouth and spouted it out at the top of its head. This mistake was cleared up as soon as scientists began to study how whales live.

RIGHT WHALE

BLUE WHALE

SPOUTS OF

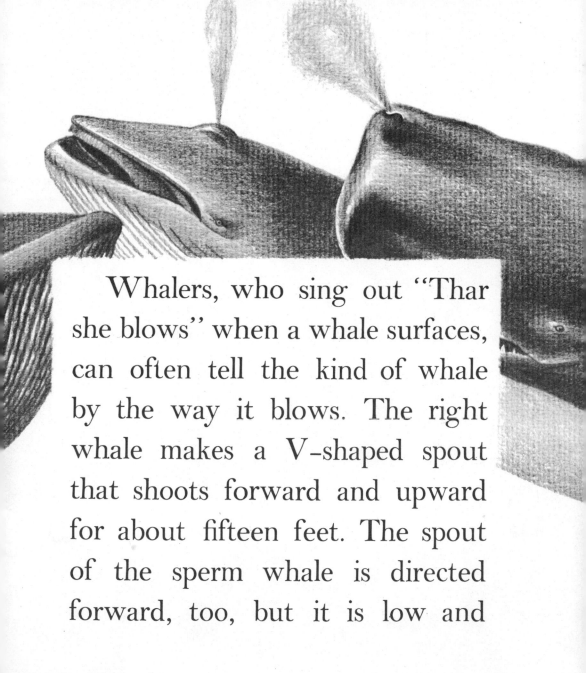

Whalers, who sing out "Thar she blows" when a whale surfaces, can often tell the kind of whale by the way it blows. The right whale makes a V–shaped spout that shoots forward and upward for about fifteen feet. The spout of the sperm whale is directed forward, too, but it is low and

WHALES

FINBACK WHALE   SPERM WHALE

bushy. The finback's spout is cone-shaped and about ten to twelve feet high. The giant blue whale blows a column twenty feet high when it comes up from a deep dive.

How some whales dive as deep as they do is a good deal of a mystery. In 1932 the telegraph cable between the Panama

Canal and Ecuador stopped work-
ing. A repair ship followed the
cable through the Pacific, search-
ing for the damage. Off the coast
of Colombia, sailors hauled up
the broken cable from a depth of
over half a mile (3240 feet).
Entangled in it was a forty-five-
foot sperm whale which had
been trapped and drowned.

PANAMA CANAL

COLOMBIA

ECUADOR

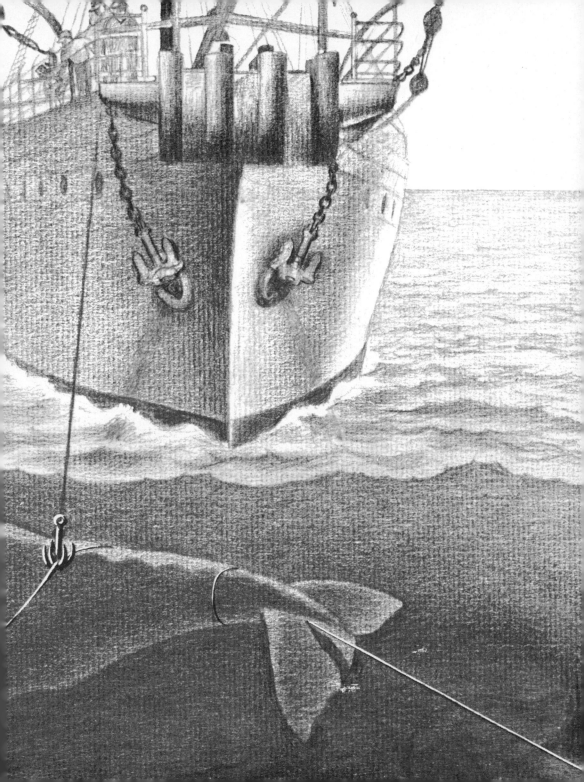

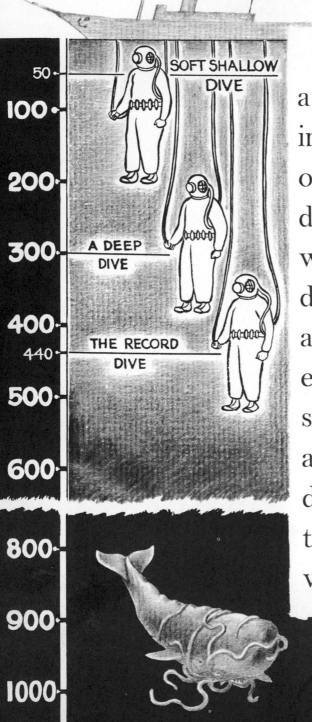

50
100
200
300
400
440
500
600
800
900
1000

SOFT SHALLOW DIVE

A DEEP DIVE

THE RECORD DIVE

The record for a man in a diving suit is a dive of 440 feet. A diver can hardly work in water as deep as 300 feet and must be raised to the surface slowly in order to avoid a pressure disease known as the bends. Most whales go down several hundred feet to feed, and perhaps much deeper. The pressure may be over a thousand pounds for every square inch of the sperm whale's great body. Yet it suffers no ill effects. This is because a whale does not breathe during its long dive. It holds its breath all the time it is under water, for periods of ten minutes up to an hour or more. It has enough oxygen in its blood to keep alive and moving all this time.

In order that a whale may stay under so long, it must replace the life-giving oxygen in its blood as soon as it reaches the surface. It does this by blowing a number of times and taking shallow rolling dives between long ones. A sperm whale may make twenty shallow dives after a deep one. The blue whale makes a dozen or more and the right whale only five or six.

SECTION THROUGH HEAD OF FINBACK WHALE SHOWING SEPARATE COURSE TAKEN BY FOOD AND AIR

BLOWHOLE

AIR

MOUTH

FOOD

WINDPIPE

ESOPHAGUS

The whale's body is adjusted to diving and to the ocean depths in many ways. Its eyes are small and are well protected in their deep sockets. The ear openings are tiny holes. The nostrils are kept closed and only open when the whale is breathing. Whenever a whale dives, it holds its breath and its heartbeat and body movements slow down. By slowing down when under water, the whale makes the best use of its supply of oxygen and can sub-

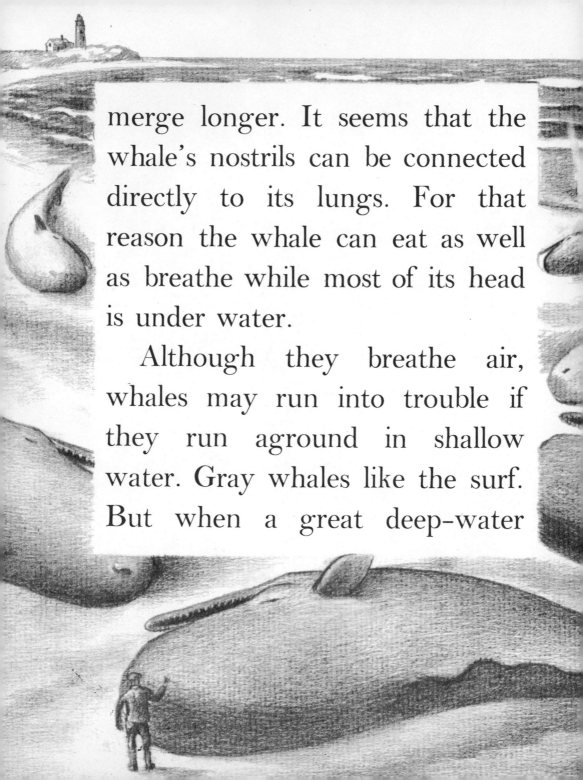

merge longer. It seems that the whale's nostrils can be connected directly to its lungs. For that reason the whale can eat as well as breathe while most of its head is under water.

Although they breathe air, whales may run into trouble if they run aground in shallow water. Gray whales like the surf. But when a great deep-water

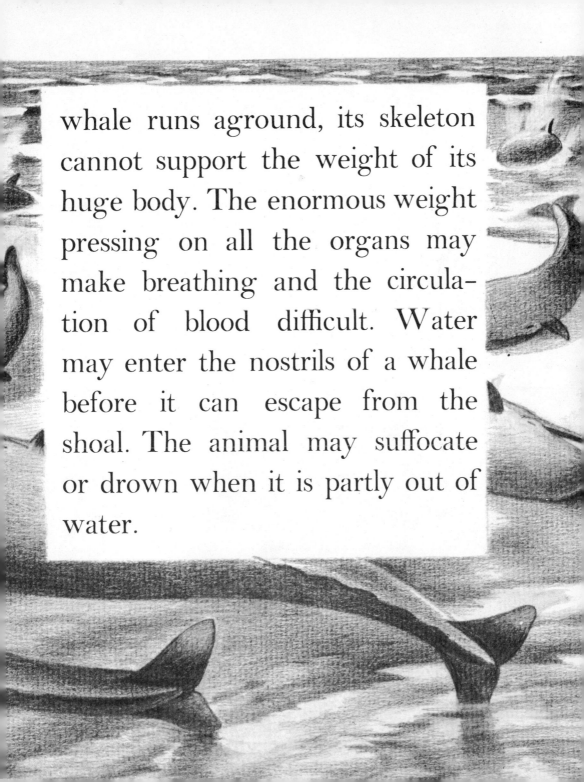

whale runs aground, its skeleton cannot support the weight of its huge body. The enormous weight pressing on all the organs may make breathing and the circulation of blood difficult. Water may enter the nostrils of a whale before it can escape from the shoal. The animal may suffocate or drown when it is partly out of water.

Whales are divided into two groups, mainly by the way they feed and the food they eat. The largest group, the toothed whales, feeds on fish and large sea animals. Some of these whales have as few as two teeth; others have fifty or more. The toothed whales have a single blowhole on top of their heads, instead of double nostrils. Most of them are small and only one, the sperm whale, reaches mammoth size.

BLOWHOLES
← WHALEBONE WHALE, DOUBLE
(HUMPBACK)
TOOTHED WHALE, ↗
SINGLE (SPERM)

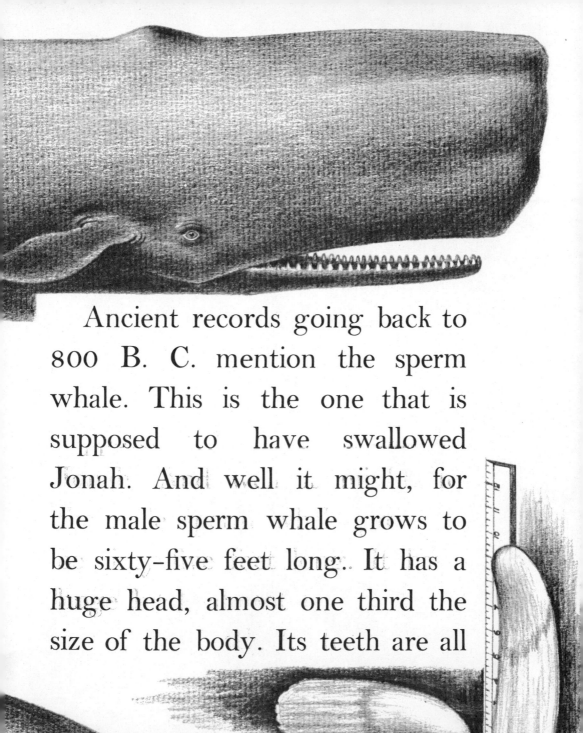

Ancient records going back to 800 B. C. mention the sperm whale. This is the one that is supposed to have swallowed Jonah. And well it might, for the male sperm whale grows to be sixty-five feet long. It has a huge head, almost one third the size of the body. Its teeth are all

SPERM WHALE TEETH

in the small lower jaw. The
sperm whale feeds on giant
squids. It could swallow a seal,
shark, or even an unlucky whaler.
In the early days of whaling it
crushed many a whaleboat in its
jaws.

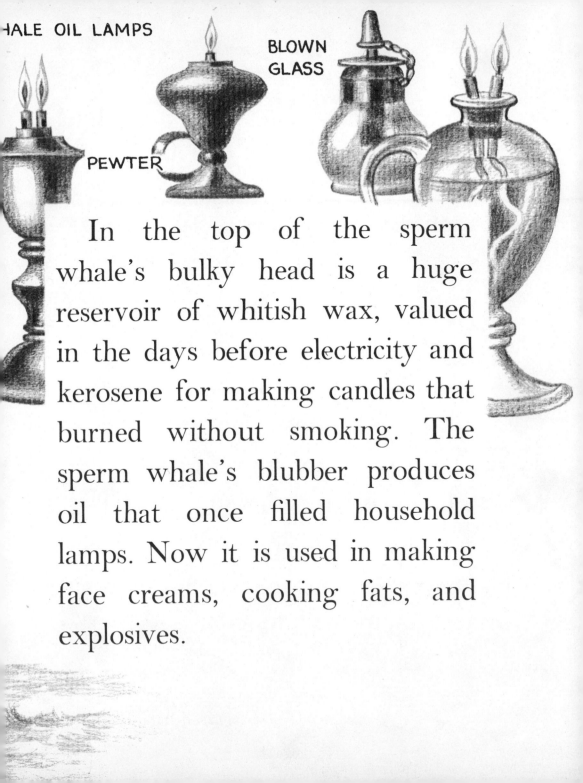

WHALE OIL LAMPS

BLOWN GLASS

PEWTER

In the top of the sperm whale's bulky head is a huge reservoir of whitish wax, valued in the days before electricity and kerosene for making candles that burned without smoking. The sperm whale's blubber produces oil that once filled household lamps. Now it is used in making face creams, cooking fats, and explosives.

The sperm whale may eat over half a ton of giant squids and other foods every day. Now and then this diet seems to disagree with the whale and a thick, grayish, greasy lump, that may weigh up to several hundred pounds, forms in its intestines. This odd substance, known as ambergris, is sometimes found when sperm whales are killed. It has occasionally been seen floating at sea or washed up on a beach. Ambergris has the

GIANT SQUID

property of making the fragrance of perfume last longer. It is extremely valuable, and a large lump may bring a fortune to the finder. But for every person who finds real ambergris, hundreds are disappointed when their finds turn out to be some other wax, grease, or refuse.

AMBERGRIS

The second group of whales is smaller in number but larger in size. These have no teeth. They include most of the great whales. All have a double nostril, or blowhole, and a huge mouth, even larger than the sperm whale's. These baleen whales have no teeth at all. Instead, several hundred sheets of baleen or whalebone hang down from the roof of the mouth in two rows, one on each side.

Whalebone is not bone at all;

RIGHT WHALE

it is a horny material something like your fingernails. The inner edges of the whalebone are frayed into bushy bristles, which make the upper jaw into a huge strainer. The blue, right, gray, finback, humpback, and bowhead whales belong in this group.

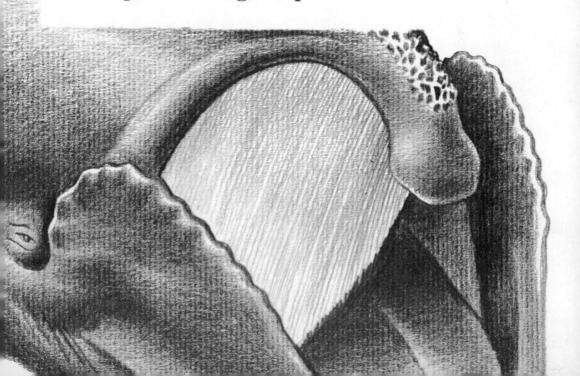

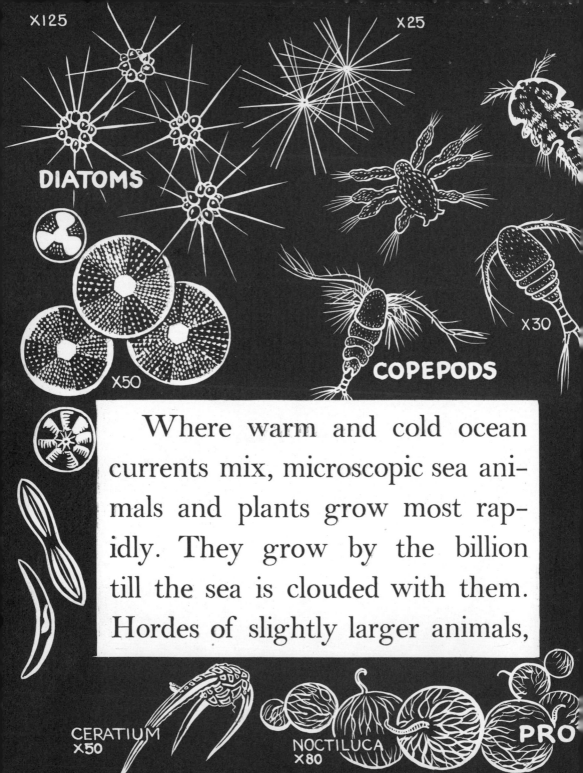

X125

X25

DIATOMS

X50

COPEPODS

X30

Where warm and cold ocean currents mix, microscopic sea animals and plants grow most rapidly. They grow by the billion till the sea is clouded with them. Hordes of slightly larger animals,

CERATIUM
X50

NOCTILUCA
X80

PRO

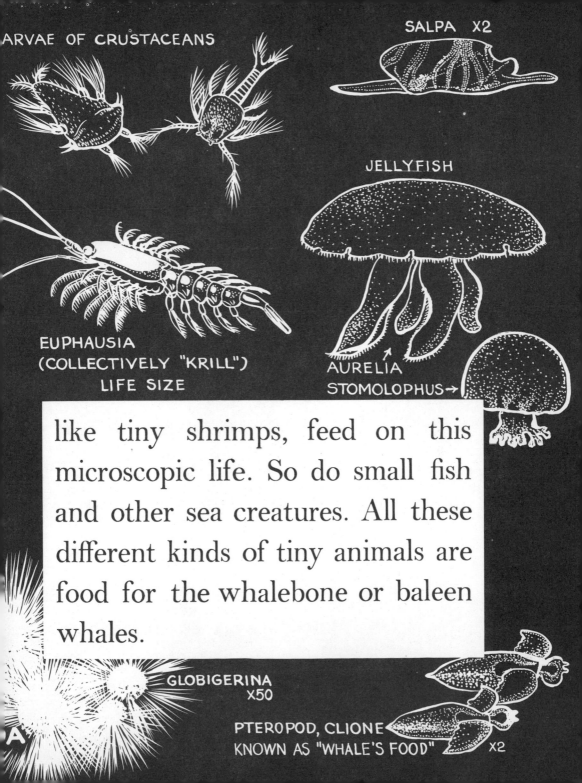

LARVAE OF CRUSTACEANS

SALPA X2

JELLYFISH

EUPHAUSIA
(COLLECTIVELY "KRILL")
LIFE SIZE

AURELIA
STOMOLOPHUS→

like tiny shrimps, feed on this microscopic life. So do small fish and other sea creatures. All these different kinds of tiny animals are food for the whalebone or baleen whales.

GLOBIGERINA
X50

A

PTEROPOD, CLIONE
KNOWN AS "WHALE'S FOOD"   X2

Through these miles of teeming ocean life, the baleen whales swim with their enormous mouths partly open. Thousands upon thousands of tiny sea animals are trapped in the rows of baleen and are eaten. The whales also feed by filling their mouths with water, closing them, and raising their tongues to force the water out through the baleen strainers. The animals thus caught are easily swallowed even though the throats of these whales are small

compared to their huge mouths.

The rapid growth of tiny water plants and shrimplike animals depends on the seasons. So the great whales find their rich supply of food in different parts of the ocean at different times of the year. They move from colder water back to warm and back again, keeping near the beds of floating food. Some whales spend the summer in the arctic or antarctic waters and move toward the tropics in winter.

BLACKFISH OR PILOT WHALE

KILLER WHALE

COMMON DOLPHIN

Besides these two groups, the whale family includes some that are not called whales. Most of these belong with the toothed whales, like the dolphins and porpoises which race alongside the bows of steamers. The com-

BOTTLENOSE DOLPHIN

NARWHAL

HARBOR PORPOISE

mon blackfish is not a fish. It is a whale. So are the narwhal, the killer, and the grampus. These and other small whales roam the oceans; a few even live in large rivers. They are small for whales, but except for the very smallest,

GRAMPUS OR
RISSO'S PORPOISE

they are larger and heavier than a six-foot man. Some may grow to be twenty-five feet long.

Most whales are sociable animals, moving and feeding in groups or schools. In winter or early spring the males and females begin to pair off. The humpback whales, perhaps more than all others, court the females.

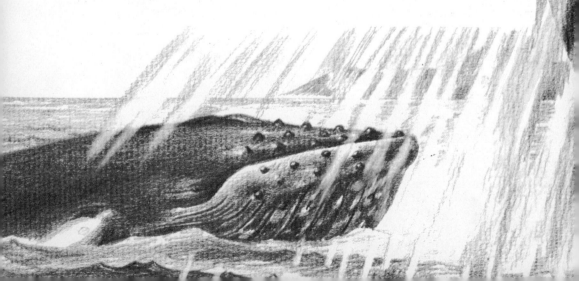

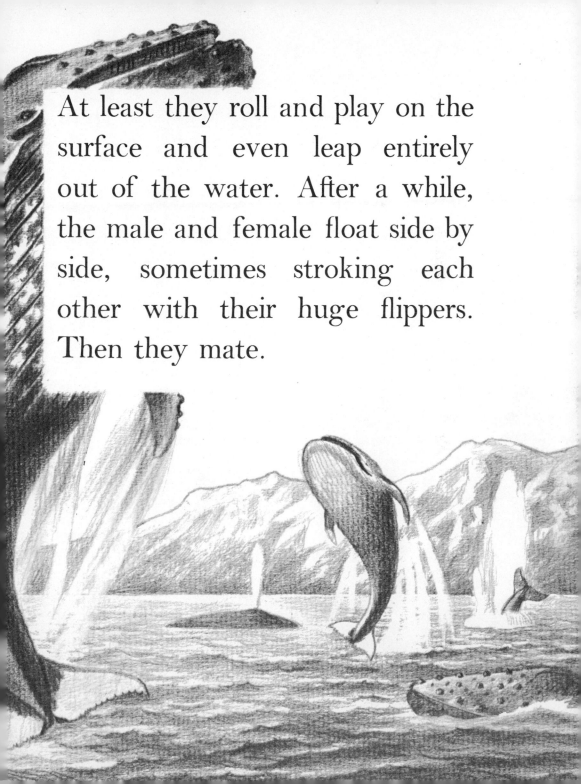

At least they roll and play on the surface and even leap entirely out of the water. After a while, the male and female float side by side, sometimes stroking each other with their huge flippers. Then they mate.

The unborn whale grows for ten or twelve months inside its mother. By the time it is born, it has reached a length of about fifteen feet and weighs about a ton. The baby blue whale may be twenty-five feet long at birth and may weigh several tons. Whales rarely have twins.

Mother whales are fond of their young. They fondle them and protect them from enemies.

Like other mammals, the baby whales are fed milk. The mother rolls on her side to feed her young. She has two nipples and the baby sucks just like a puppy or kitten. The mother helps by squeezing the milk into the baby's mouth. The baby is nursed for seven months to a year, depending on the kind of whale. During this time it grows rapidly. It is not unusual for a baby whale to double its length in a single year. In about three years it is full-grown. A blue whale may grow to be fifty feet long by the time it is one year old. Some whales live only eight or ten years; other kinds live twice as long and perhaps even longer.

GROWTH OF A BLUE WHALE

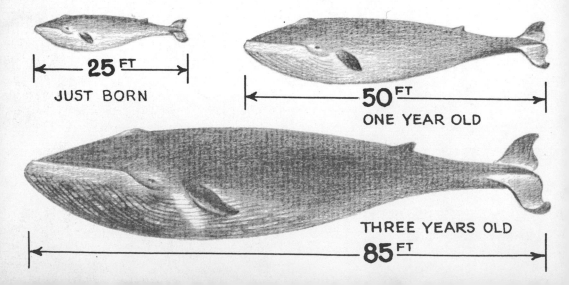

25 FT
JUST BORN

50 FT
ONE YEAR OLD

THREE YEARS OLD
85 FT

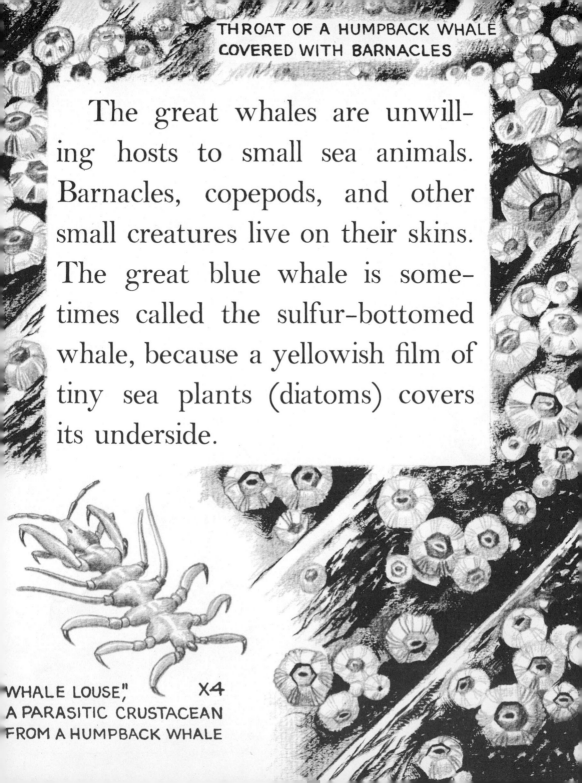

The great whales are unwilling hosts to small sea animals. Barnacles, copepods, and other small creatures live on their skins. The great blue whale is sometimes called the sulfur-bottomed whale, because a yellowish film of tiny sea plants (diatoms) covers its underside.

WHALE LOUSE," X4
A PARASITIC CRUSTACEAN
FROM A HUMPBACK WHALE

Because of their size the giant whales have few enemies. One which the great whales seem to know and fear is a smaller whale called the killer. These twenty-foot sea wolves travel in packs and sometimes attack even the largest

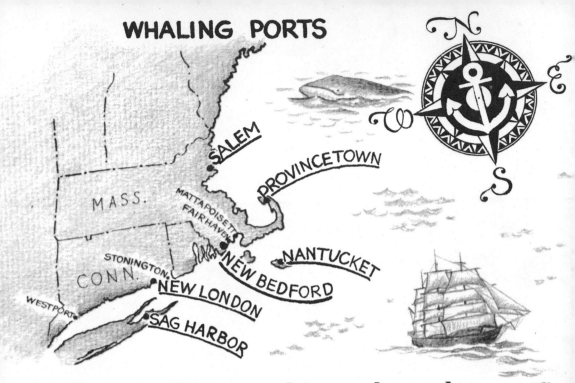

WHALING PORTS

whales. But nothing that the ferocious killers do can compare with what man has done to the whales. Men have hunted and killed whales for centuries. In the early days of this country, whaling was an important industry.

Ships sailed from New Bedford and other whaling ports on voyages that lasted several years. Harpooning and killing the whale was hard and dangerous work. But each year more and more whales were killed.

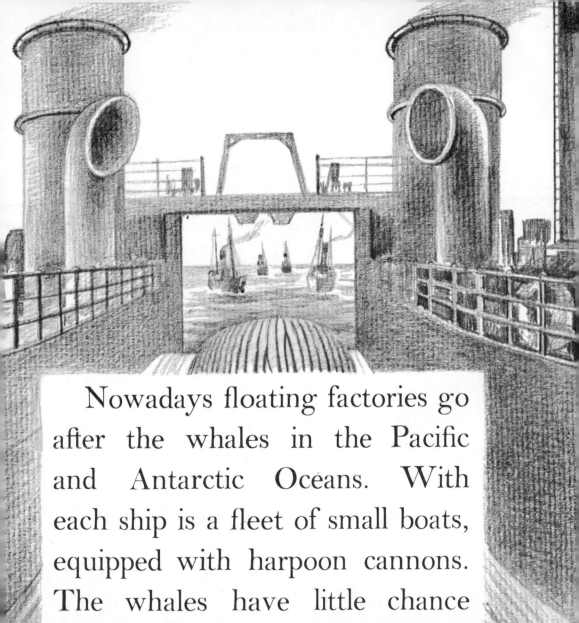

Nowadays floating factories go after the whales in the Pacific and Antarctic Oceans. With each ship is a fleet of small boats, equipped with harpoon cannons. The whales have little chance against such deadly weapons, and

whalers are able to kill most of the whales they can find.

As whales became scarce, the leading nations made treaties to protect them and to set aside regions where they cannot be hunted. Even with this protec-

All baleen whales protected from factory ship whaling: ▉
Taking of baleen whales by factory ship permitted: ⧄
Antarctic Regions: Whaleships permitted to operate for baleen whales within limits. The 1949-1950 Season was from December 22 to April 7, and a limit of 1250 was placed on Humpbacks: ⧄ Shore stations can operate anywhere in the world with a six months' season.

tion, the whales are losing ground. Scientists say that unless we protect whales even more, these largest of all mammals may become rare. Some kinds may become as extinct as the largest of all reptiles, the dinosaurs.

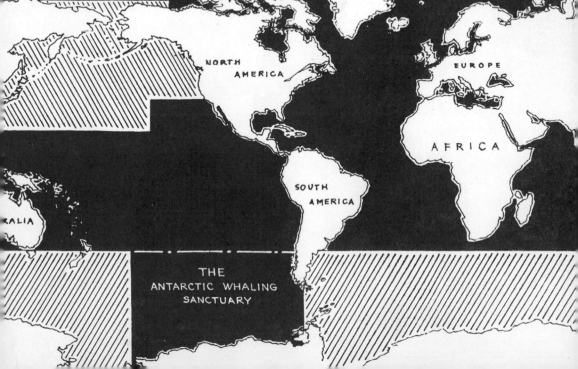

GREENLAND

NORTH AMERICA

EUROPE

AFRICA

SOUTH AMERICA

RALIA

THE ANTARCTIC WHALING SANCTUARY

Thanks are due to Dr. Raymond M. Gilmore,
Office of Foreign Affairs,
United States Fish and Wildlife Service,
for reading and criticizing the manuscript.

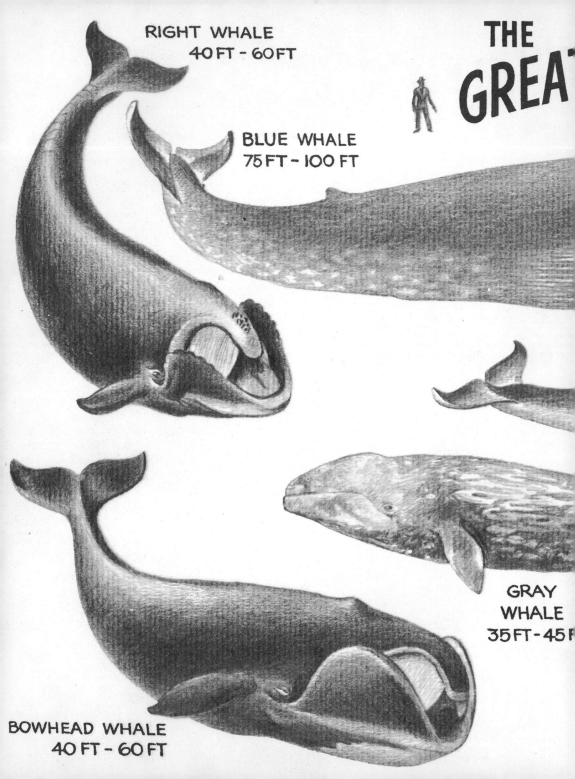

RIGHT WHALE
40 FT - 60 FT

BLUE WHALE
75 FT - 100 FT

THE
GREAT

GRAY
WHALE
35 FT - 45 F

BOWHEAD WHALE
40 FT - 60 FT

WHALES

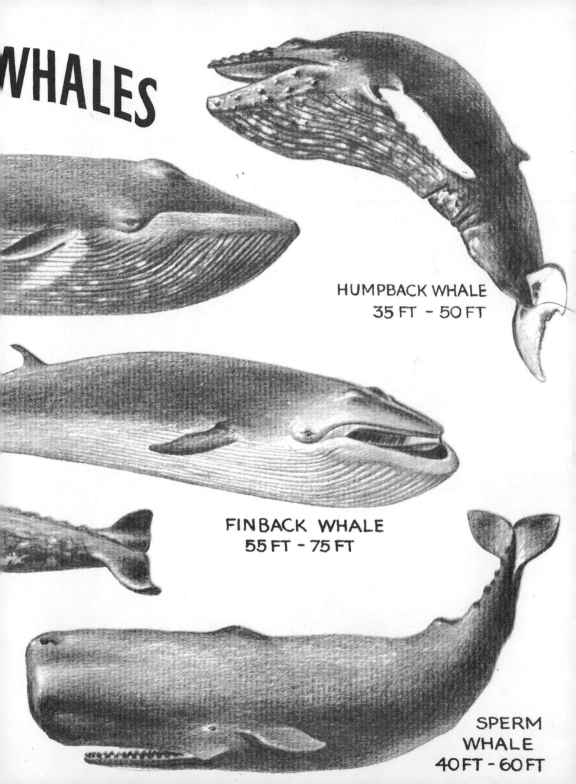

HUMPBACK WHALE
35 FT – 50 FT

FINBACK WHALE
55 FT – 75 FT

SPERM
WHALE
40 FT – 60 FT